The Knowledge Net

A REPORT OF THE NEW EXPEDITIONS INITIATIVE

Connecting Communities, Learners, and Colleges

American Association of Community Colleges

Association of Community College Trustees

with support from the

W. K. Kellogg Foundation

Community College Press®

a division of the

American Association of

Community Colleges

Washington, D.C.

The American Association of Community Colleges (AACC) is the primary advocacy organization for the nation's community colleges. The association represents 1,100 two-year, associate degree–granting institutions and some 10 million students. AACC provides leadership and service in five key areas: policy initiatives, advocacy, research, education services, and coordination/networking.

Requests for permission should be sent to
Community College Press
American Association of Community Colleges
One Dupont Circle, NW
Suite 410
Washington, DC 20036
Fax: (202) 223-9390

Printed in the United States of America.

ISBN 0-87117-329-8

Contents

Preface

The New Expeditions initiative was launched in April 1998 as a joint project of the American Association of Community Colleges and the Association of Community College Trustees. The W. K. Kellogg Foundation supported the effort to consider current issues and to offer a vision for the future of community colleges.

The New Expeditions Coordinating Committee—comprising the executive boards of the two national associations—sought the input of educators, students, trustees, business and community leaders, and other stakeholders around the nation. Over a 12-month period, the committee commissioned research papers, sought verbal and written viewpoints, and sponsored 39 public hearings, focus groups, and community conversations across the country. The New Expeditions Web site conveyed information and solicited opinions. *The Knowledge Net* is the result of these efforts.

The public and private institutions discussed in this report answer to many names, including college, junior college, community college, technical college, state college, tribal college, and institute. The report represents all regionally accredited institutions that grant the associate degree as their highest degree as well as those that grant one or more degrees beyond the associate degree but choose to associate themselves with community colleges. *The Knowledge Net* is intended to serve as an agenda for the first part of the 21st century for all these institutions, collectively referred to here as community colleges. Although this work will be of interest to many readers, it is directed first and foremost to community college chief executive officers.

This report was made possible by the generous support of many individuals and organizations, particularly the W. K. Kellogg Foundation through Betty Overton-Adkins and Delores Parker. Profound thanks go to the New Expeditions Coordinating Committee members and chair Robert Atwell for their invaluable vision, guidance, and direction, and to Madeline Patton for her tireless efforts in drafting the report. We extend our gratitude to the following people and organizations who helped organize focus groups, public hearings, and community conversations: Barry Garron, Catherine Ann Reed, Claire Gauntlett, Iris Heavyrunner, and Gerry Bazer. Others who offered thoughtful insight include Edmund J. Gleazer and Dale Parnell. Special thanks go to staff, including Lynn Barnett, J. Noah Brown, and Dibya Sarkar, without whose efforts the New Expeditions project and this report would not have been possible. The list of contributors includes the names of other organizations and people whose valuable insights helped shape the project and the report. On behalf of the New Expeditions Initiative, to all who expressed interest and gave their time, we express our sincere appreciation.

David R. Pierce
President
American Association of
Community Colleges

Ray Taylor
President
Association of Community College
Trustees

Coordinating Committee

Introduction

The 1988 landmark report *Building Communities* defined *community* "not only as a region to be served, but also as a climate to be created." As community, junior, and technical colleges approach their second century of service, this clarion call continues. Communities across the United States face constant challenges that require educational institutions to respond and point the way. In a society facing unparalleled and accelerating change, the most important challenge for community colleges is to help shape that change. The colleges must provide opportunities for people to become all they are capable of being. The community college mission to serve and to create a climate for change is still relevant as the new century dawns.

If anything, the stakes are higher now than ever before. Biogenetics, aging baby boomers, increasingly mobile populations, and an ever-broadening chasm between rich and poor bring mind-boggling challenges and opportunities. The impact of technology on work and learning and the growing interdependence of world economies together create a tumultuous climate in which people increasingly look to their community colleges for help in navigating the constant ebb and flow of change.

Technology and globalization combine to further divide the haves and the have-nots—those with the skills and adaptability to navigate change and exploit opportunity and those for whom change means disruption, displacement, and detachment. Surviving and thriving in a changing world require that community colleges connect in multiple ways. They must create a network of pathways enabling people to transverse the maze successfully and profitably. To sustain these travelers in their journeys, colleges must help impart the knowledge people need to make the right decisions and choose the road that enables them to realize their potential. This is the network, *the knowledge net*, the nexus of pathways leading to empowerment through the acquisition of knowledge and the honing of skills that permit people to exploit change successfully.

In the 21st century, community colleges must strengthen the knowledge net, constantly adding new strands and ensuring that unforeseen challenges do not threaten to sever the colleges' vital community connections. To remain viable, community colleges must ensure that their programs and services are relevant, responsive, proactive, and creative. They must use their community presence to embrace and enhance diversity and inclusion. The colleges should prepare people to live and contribute in a democracy and should adhere to the principles of sound institutional citizenship. The colleges need to help people develop the skills, including cultural and language competencies, needed for success in the global marketplace. They should focus on learners. Community colleges must continue to provide the vision and leadership required to help their communities remain vital and nurturing places. In short, community colleges must connect with communities, connect with learners, and connect internally to ensure that the knowledge net is unbroken.

CHAPTER 1

Community Connections

"The purpose of education," said Ernest Boyer, "is to empower individuals to live with competence in their communities." Community college efforts to achieve this clear, powerful goal begin with connecting to their communities. Communities in the broadest sense—where people live, socialize, work, worship, raise families, recreate, learn, shop, share common goals, and transact business—vary greatly. Sometimes vast differences in wealth, education, abilities, perceptions of security, and personal characteristics are part of the heterogeneous character of the United States.

Community colleges, committed to serving all segments of their diverse communities, beckon and welcome everyone to gather in a spirit of neutrality, safety, hope, and aspiration. In some places, the multiple roles community colleges play make them the most important institution in the community. People come to community colleges for many reasons: to pursue a degree, to develop skills for satisfying employment, to participate in community forums or recreational or cultural activities, or just to experience the joy of learning. Communities in distress may call upon their colleges to serve as mediators, unifiers, or even rescuers. Although most programs and services may be familiar and routine, change is constant and community needs evolve. As the official links to the community, college chief executive officers and governing boards must ensure that the institution serves all segments of the community. These include the civic sector, employer community, and other educational entities.

THE CIVIC ROLE

A democracy depends on people knowing how they connect to their community, state, and nation. Citizens must have a sense of civic duty and an understanding of the rights and responsibilities of citizenship. Those who are not citizens should have, at minimum, an understanding of how communities make decisions and how even noncitizens can participate in civic life. Community colleges help

RECOMMENDATIONS

■ Community colleges should use their widespread community prominence and accessibility to help forge positive relationships among diverse segments of society.

■ Community colleges should assess their community's needs and assets and implement appropriate programs to cultivate and enhance current and future community leaders.

■ Community colleges should provide learners with an array of experiences to help them gain civic awareness and skills that will enhance their participation in a democracy.

■ Community colleges should be exemplary institutional citizens and leaders in their communities.

■ Community colleges should encourage staff and students to become active participants in community activities.

■ Community colleges should support the arts in their communities, foster partnerships that support cultural events, and strengthen programming when the college serves as the community's cultural focus.

citizens and immigrants to contribute through educational and community programs. The colleges can and should be models of civic leadership.

Common Ground

As places that enjoy the trust and confidence of the community at large, community colleges represent a common ground for people with differing views, experiences, or heritage. Because the public perceives community colleges to be neutral ground, where anyone is welcome, they are safe places to confront tough issues. Over the years many of them have

done just that. They can and should continue to use their status to convene groups whose viewpoints differ. They should not shy from opportunities for problem solving, even when the issues to be confronted are as varied and contentious as hate crimes or rural land development. As catalysts, community colleges can stimulate collaboration and the development of partnerships that will encourage citizen engagement. As conveners, they also can help lead celebrations for those who have made positive contributions to their communities.

As human behavior in American society seems increasingly conflict driven, community colleges need to strengthen their role as conveners of community members. Communities should view their colleges as safe places for people to explore and appreciate differences and to find solutions when conflict arises. The diversity of community college learners enriches the educational experience, promotes personal growth, and strengthens communities and the workplace. The inclusiveness of community colleges leads to a healthy society. Community colleges provide places on and off campus where people can express concerns about issues ranging from racial problems to work-

Common ground. In the midst of citywide riots, East Los Angeles Community College was one of the few places left untouched. To head off further violence, the college hosted and mediated meetings of rival gang members. Jackson Community College, Michigan, is developing a Citizen Center for the Common Good, a community-based incubator for social innovation and entrepreneurship.

place strife. Harmony must come from learning about each other and learning how to appreciate differences in ways that do not compel conformity.

Community Leadership

Community colleges have a vested interest in developing local leaders since most of their constituents live and remain in the community. Community college graduates often hold leadership positions in the community. Every community has invisible human resources—people who are not

> *Developing community leaders.* The Citizen Leadership Institute at Gulf Coast Community College, Florida, uses a curriculum of motivation and skill-building to cultivate action-oriented, grassroots citizen leaders. Richland College, Texas, partners with the Chamber of Commerce in the Dallas area's prestigious Leadership Richardson, a yearlong program for emerging and experienced community leaders, including college administrators.

in obvious leadership positions or who might not consider themselves to be leaders. Community colleges, alone or in collaboration with other groups, owe it to their communities to develop the skills, knowledge, and motivation of these future leaders. They should look for hidden potential in all corners of their communities, discovering young and old who aspire to building better places to live. Colleges can offer mentoring programs, summer camps, yearlong leadership-training programs, small-group instruction in leadership skills, and other efforts that help develop people as leaders.

Skills for a Democracy

Because public distrust and disillusionment in recent years have led to a breakdown in citizen participation, it is incumbent upon community colleges to help cultivate habits and attitudes for active citizenship. Citizenship is about more than guaranteed rights; it is about responsibility—a fact many people forget. Citizens want the right to a trial by jury, for instance, but often seek ways to avoid serving on a jury themselves. They want the right to criticize politicians but not the responsibility of determining who gains public office. Communities must expand efforts to increase citizen participation, such as encouraging voter turnout and service on juries. Colleges should inform their students and personnel of opportunities for direct participation in issues that are important to them. Many community colleges have embraced service and other community-based learning as a way for students to serve their communities while acquiring an education. Expansion of these programs should be encouraged. People learn citizenship best by doing, and options for service should be a common expectation of colleges and their communities.

Part of any community college's role must be to develop learners' civic skills as well as to build their occupational skills. As the educators of more than 10 million people annually, community colleges are primed to help build a nation of people with the skills needed for an effectively functioning democracy. Unfettered,

> *"Never doubt that a small group of thoughtful citizens can change the world; indeed, it is the only thing that ever has."*
> —*Margaret Mead*

Civic responsibility. Miami-Dade Community College, Florida, pilots Forums on Civic Responsibility. Students write letters to themselves stating what they are willing do to be a better citizen. In an Oakton (Illinois) Community College course, "The Civic Mind," service learning students research social problems in the community. Students in the One America program at Glendale Community College, California, organize events on civic issues for college and community members.

yet civil, dialogue is part of the learning process. Community colleges should strengthen efforts to help people communicate and interact in positive ways, learn to listen, mediate differences, facilitate discussions, work in teams, and resolve conflicts. This kind of learning can take place in regular classrooms as well as in college-sponsored community programs. Openness, civility, and inclusiveness must be the hallmarks of such programs.

Institutional Citizenship

Just as community colleges seek to build the values of good citizenship in their students, they have an obligation to be good citizens themselves. This can mean something as routine as compliance with federal regulations such as those of the Occupational Safety and Health Administration or the Americans with Disabilities Act. But institutional citizenship means much more than obeying laws. It also requires a degree of altruism. Most community colleges rightly engage in external issues that directly affect learning. They should choose activities based on the expertise or resources they can offer to help solve a community's

problems and to improve the quality of life for its members. Colleges should encourage their personnel to become active community members and support their volunteer efforts.

Institutional citizenship means thinking big. More than any other institution, a community college has to think beyond its own doors. It cannot sit back and wait for someone else to solve problems. Those problems could permeate the college within a single generation. The consequences of children without immunizations, homes without heat, and neighborhoods without public transportation, for example, touch an entire community sooner or later. People without access to computers or transportation quickly fall behind. Community college leaders must assume responsibility for becoming part of the solution. No longer can anyone rationalize that health is irrel-

Institutional citizenship. When the floods of Hurricane Floyd devastated North Carolina in 1999, Lenoir, Edgecombe, and Pitt Community Colleges led efforts to help college and community members recover and start fresh. Lenoir served as a Red Cross emergency shelter.

evant to learning or that what happens to preschoolers or the elderly does not affect a community's quality of life.

Finally, in their interactions with personnel, learners, and the general public, community colleges need to practice the skills they are teaching. These skills include collaborating, listening, facilitating, systems thinking, and consensus building.

Encouraging the Arts

The fine arts, as an expression of human

creativity and freedom, hold a special place in a democracy, and community colleges help maintain that place. Many community colleges, particularly in rural areas, serve as centers for the arts—in fact,

Arts and culture. The professional dance company in residence at Howard Community College, Maryland, performs and tours with professional, community, and student members. Southeast Community College, Kentucky, preserves mountain history through its Appalachian Center and the Kentucky Coal Mine Museum. Sinte Gleska University, South Dakota, preserves tribal artifacts in a new facility, and Alabama Southern Community College honors Southern writers at its annual literary festival.

they sometimes provide the only cultural activity in town. In other communities, college art centers supplement public- and private-sector programs. They give voice and visibility to fledgling and experienced artists and craftspeople, and they attract new and veteran audiences. Whether a specialized museum or citywide book fair, craft show, or television station, a special cultural seminar or art gallery, or a theater or concert, the arts programming hosted by community colleges meets a local need and broadens perspectives. Most colleges have some of these programs; others have all of them and more.

Although the degree to which an institution can address all of the programs varies, every college should view support of the arts not only as a community service but also as an effective community connector. At every opportunity, community colleges should welcome partnerships

that bring the arts to life in ways that benefit all members of the communities. They are part of the knowledge net.

EMPLOYERS AND THE ECONOMY

An insufficient and underskilled workforce threatens a nation's economy. Today's employers report difficulty attracting and retaining skilled workers, and the shortage is expected to worsen. As aging baby boomers retire and the workforce shrinks, colleges can expect a talent war for skilled workers. Future economic growth depends on people's working smarter, not just harder, and the role of community colleges in this area is more important now than ever. With the rapid expansion of private-sector interest in education and training, community colleges must perform in an increasingly competitive environment. Those who do not respond competitively will lose students and contracts to organizations that can provide services unencumbered by debates about scheduling, academic freedom, or seat time.

Workforce Development

Technological advances in the workplace call for workers with complex skills to fill jobs that previously did not require postsecondary education. Just a generation ago, many jobs did not require even basic literacy. An unskilled worker with strength and stamina could command middle-class wages. Today's skilled workers must be part of the knowledge net—fluent in technology as well as communication and team skills.

Technology has flattened the organizational structure of the workplace, requiring people to be more adept at functioning in groups, analyzing problems, and making decisions without a supervisor's direct involvement. Critical thinking, interper-

RECOMMENDATIONS

■ Community colleges should view the preparation and development of the nation's workforce as a primary part of their mission and communicate to policymakers the uniqueness of this community college role.

■ Community colleges must view basic literacy, English-as-a-second-language, and remedial programs as essential parts of their mission with positive effects on democracy and economic life.

■ Community colleges should provide people with the academic, technical, and workplace social skills necessary for successful careers.

■ Community colleges should expand services to support emerging, existing, transitional, and entrepreneurial workers.

■ Community colleges should meet regularly with employers to establish processes for timely curricular, policy, and scheduling revisions that reflect new regulations or changing market needs and practices.

■ Community colleges should collaborate with public and private human resource providers to reduce duplication and optimize coordination of services.

■ Community colleges should develop strategic plans for global awareness and competence that respond to the needs of their community's learners, businesses, and institutions.

■ Community colleges should increase and expand programs for global understanding, including language and culture, that will help connect the various cultures in their own communities.

sonal competence, and computer literacy have joined reading, writing, and computing as basic skills. Intercultural and international understanding are fast

Workforce training. On New York's Wall Street, Borough of Manhattan Community College faculty teach business management degree courses to Salomon Smith Barney employees. The company makes tuition payments directly to the college. El Paso Community College, Texas, has a bilingual program to train workers for new jobs after being displaced by the North American Free Trade Agreement.

becoming part of that required skill set. To successfully sustain and adapt their careers to market fluctuations, workers must have a solid educational foundation and be ready to learn more throughout their lives. Because of the pace of change, lifelong learning is a necessity for continued employment. For this reason, community colleges should view everything they do as part of workforce development, from traditional transfer programs that lead to a bachelor's degree to English-as-a-second-language programs, remedial education, occupational skills training, and noncredit certification courses.

Adjusting to the Marketplace

Community colleges face a challenge similar to the one confronting businesses: how to meet current and future market demands. National surveys indicate that every job sector, including community colleges, expects to retrain workers on a regular basis. Each community college should determine the needs of its area business and industry and respond to them. Colleges must include themselves in local surveys. Increasingly, colleges will find it difficult to recruit, retain, and pay full-time or part-time faculty, especially

Meeting market needs. Springfield Technical Community College, Massachusetts, established the Springfield Enterprise Center with an unusual business incubator. In addition to space for 20 new startup businesses, its Youth Incubator has room and services to support new business development by teens. Spearheaded by Central Piedmont Community College, North Carolina, the Workforce Development Continuum in Charlotte brings education, business, and government sectors together to give workers learning opportunities and skills certifications.

in the areas of mathematics, science, engineering, and technology. Colleges that are attuned to workforce development needs will expand services for incumbent workers, those in transition, and those who are entrepreneurs.

Ideally, community colleges' response to local needs will be coordinated with other private and public providers of human development services to avoid unproductive duplication. Colleges should expand collaborations with the business community and should be careful not to present their institutions as the presumptive deliverers of all higher education services. Collaborative approaches usually result in a higher-quality, better-prepared workforce. College-business partnerships can provide colleges with access to labs, equipment, and expertise to strengthen educational programs and enhance overall service to the community.

The Global Village

Economic forces and high-tech communications connect people throughout the world. As these connections become commonplace, it is essential that individuals understand what *global village* means. A basic understanding of the world's nations and the people who populate them is a necessity in the international market, and community colleges must develop strategies to enhance each learner's global awareness.

Just as each institution must know what *general education* means, so too must it have a vision for its international education programs. The vision can be as basic as wanting all learners to understand the interconnected nature of the world they live in, including options for learning different languages or studying various cultures. Or a college may have more complex aspirations. It may envision providing import and export information to area businesses, training local people for jobs in other countries, or working directly with people, businesses, governments, or institutions in other countries. A college's international and intercultural vision must include learners in occupational as well as transfer programs. The assumption that success in an occupational program

Global awareness. Kapi`olani Community College, Hawaii, has an Asian-Pacific emphasis across the curriculum. Utah Valley State College students increased their vocabulary and diplomatic skills on study-abroad trips to China, and Johnson County (Kansas) Community College's students and faculty spend spring break on community service learning projects in Mexico. Crowder College students in rural Missouri have international Internet pen pals.

requires no language or cultural awareness is shortsighted for the community and for individual learners. Goals and programs should follow the vision while connecting to local priorities. History holds many examples of well-intended international programs that ran aground due to lack of local support.

To be successful, an international studies or global studies program should be crafted around the needs of the community's learners, businesses, and institutions and involve a broad representation of the college's constituency. If program choices align with this principle, the program will win support and flourish. If not, the odds of failure are high.

P–16 CONNECTIONS

Access to higher education requires not only open-admissions policies but also a coordinated effort to eliminate academic and attitudinal barriers that begin even

RECOMMENDATIONS

■ Community colleges should develop partnerships and programs that help preschool through secondary school youth prepare for a lifetime of learning.

■ Community colleges and universities should develop partnerships that ease academic and personal transitions to baccalaureate and graduate-level education.

■ Community colleges should fortify their role in preparing K–12 teachers by strengthening their science, mathematics, engineering, and technology programs.

■ Community colleges should offer quality programs for teacher professional development.

before elementary school. Education must progress seamlessly from preschool through college.

Early Childhood Education
To fulfill the commitment to lifelong learning, community colleges must look beyond their traditional age boundaries, because the key to success is teaching children how to learn and how to interact with people. Research indicates that the years before a child reaches kindergarten are pivotal to the learning process. Problems in early childhood education usually follow an individual into later education and the workplace. The foundation of basic education cannot be underestimated. Community colleges have many opportunities to play a significant role in early education through quality daycare

> *"Poverty has a greater negative impact on the ability of a young child's brain to focus, organize, and problem-solve than exposure to cocaine before birth, according to U.S. researchers."*
> —Journal of Developmental and Behavioral Pediatrics

programs on their own campuses, read-aloud and tutoring services, preparation of qualified Even Start and Head Start instructors and aides, adopt-a-school programs, and others. They should take these opportunities seriously.

Elementary and Secondary Education
The quality of a student's previous school experience strongly influences persistence in higher education for all students, but especially for African American and Hispanic students. Because early course choices affect students' decisions about their high school curriculum, community

Reaching youth. Middle-school girls learn basic electrical engineering concepts during summer workshops at Portland Community College, Oregon. In Houston, Project GRAD incorporates reading, writing, and math programs with student discipline and parent involvement. Calhoun State Community College, Alabama, and Lake Michigan have longstanding adopt-a-school programs that encourage youth to plan for college.

colleges need to start connecting with youngsters in elementary and middle schools. Falling behind in reading, math, and science in these early years of schooling makes it difficult for students to take college-prep courses in high school. Students coming underprepared to community colleges will not progress as well as they could, and they will have fewer options for advancement than those who come prepared.

Community programs that bring youngsters to campus help make the community college a part of their world. In-school talks by college personnel raise student awareness of possibilities as students begin to think of themselves as college material and learn the academic requirements for particular careers. Many students and their parents think the basic high school graduation requirements will be enough for college and do not realize that taking challenging math and science courses increases chances of post-secondary success.

In addition to early and frequent contact, community colleges can expand their dual, or concurrent, enrollment programs to provide secondary students with curricula and facilities not offered by

their high schools. The college practice of offering courses in high schools helps ease social hurdles for teens, especially when the program offers mentoring. Tech Prep and school-to-career programs similarly bridge the gap from high school to college. Community colleges can work with local schools, businesses, and social service agencies to develop ways for students to use their nonschool time more effectively. Opening technology and recreational facilities to the community can draw otherwise disengaged youth to the campus.

Colleges and Universities

In most states, articulation agreements between community colleges and senior institutions facilitate the transfer of credits. Stronger agreements are needed, however. Further progress requires more interaction between faculties to ensure smooth transfer from one college to another. Uniform course numbering helps, as does the coordination of material to be covered in courses.

New partnerships between community colleges and four-year institutions eliminate some physical barriers between them. Shared facilities and university courses offered at community colleges allow some students to move directly into

College partnerships. Virginia's community colleges have arranged with Old Dominion University to offer the last two years of bachelor's degrees at all of the colleges. Programs vary by college to meet local needs. In partnerships with community colleges in six states, Ohio-based Franklin University offers business, technology, and allied health programs through the Internet.

a baccalaureate program without having to leave the region. Some institutions are exploring how to help transfer students manage childcare, transportation, and other challenges in a new setting. Technology widens opportunities for all students through Web-based and other distance learning courses delivered by a traditional college or university or a new virtual university.

Teacher Preparation

At a time when school enrollments are rising rapidly and public school teachers are leaving their profession in high rates, many for retirement and some out of frustration, too many public schools do not meet the quality standards needed for success in today's world. Community colleges can play a pivotal role in changing this situation. They can encourage top students to consider teaching as a career and develop partnership programs that will help those students complete the necessary degrees and certification. As teaching colleges and learner-centered institutions, community colleges can model excellence in teaching, including active and participatory learning strategies.

Often the only training elementary or middle-school teachers receive in science,

Teacher preparation. J. Sargeant Reynolds Community College, Virginia, works with other state colleges, universities, and local school districts to strengthen teacher training in math and science. Students visit precollege classrooms with "master teachers." Tulsa Community College's Parateacher Program in Oklahoma recruits people from nontraditional groups for teaching careers.

mathematics, engineering, and technology is in a community college. The colleges should strengthen these programs and encourage students to enroll in them. Community colleges should expand professional development programs for K–12 teachers—helping teachers apply technology to instruction, for example.

For the quality of teacher training to improve, it is imperative that community colleges and universities collaborate more closely. Because so many teachers begin their postsecondary education at community colleges, policymakers and educators must acknowledge and support the need for greater coordination between community colleges and senior institutions.

CHAPTER 2

Learner Connections

Five years ago this section would most likely have been titled "Student Connections." The mission statements of most community colleges have students as a priority, but higher education is in the midst of a movement to realign the focus from teaching to learning. The change is more than semantics. It is a shift from a producer-driven, or faculty-directed, endeavor to one that is consumer driven, or learner centered.

LEARNER-CENTERED COLLEGES

Higher education traditionally has measured its quality by input measures such as admissions selectivity, books in the library, and terminal degrees of the faculty. These measures have never worked well with community colleges and their traditions of open access and service to community. Recent years have seen a movement toward students' accomplish-

ments and measuring the objectives they attain and the skills they master. Community colleges should research and understand better the different learning styles of their students to ensure that all of them get the most from their college time and experiences. The learning college movement is particularly applicable to community colleges, where many students do not aspire to an associate degree or transfer to a senior institution.

Focusing on learners. Palomar College, California, revised its vision and mission statements in 1991 to focus on student learning and a partners-in-learning environment. The college promotes collaborative learning, learning communities, focus on learning outcomes, and better use of technology. Other colleges—including the Community College of Denver, Maricopa Community College District in Arizona, Lane in Oregon and Jackson Community College in Michigan—have undertaken similar efforts to become learner-centered colleges.

Community colleges have a tremendous opportunity to lead higher education in this new student-centered model of quality, with its institutional focus on learning and student success.

ACCESS AND EQUITY

From the beginning, community colleges have made access and equity nonnegotiable commitments. Providing access for all learners remains the highest priority for community colleges. Community colleges welcome all high school graduates and people who complete the general equivalency development (GED) test. They offer low-cost courses, evening and weekend courses, and courses at multiple outreach locations around the community. Distance learning offerings, also low cost, accommodate the demanding personal schedules of diverse groups of learners. As remarkable as they are, these efforts are not enough.

The country is full of people who have not approached their local community college alone, who assume they cannot afford it, who live too far from a campus, or who cannot imagine being college material. For some, a friend or relative's encouragement may have changed their minds; perhaps a chance encounter with a stranger at the right moment spurred them on. Too many unemployed or underemployed people still need education and training but do not go after it. Community colleges should find these individuals and help them reach their potential.

The rapid pace of technological change adds a significant access challenge. The World Wide Web opens the door to new learning and communication opportunities, but only for those who can access it. Members of the community who do not have computers, computer skills, or Internet access cannot connect

Redefining access. Through its Family and Community Development Center, Fort Peck Community College, Montana, reaches potential students by addressing family problems that hamper enrollment or persistence. Walters State Community College, Tennessee, and South Texas Community College use small tuition stipends and personal attention to attract dislocated workers and others to a new information technology program.

to that world. They see no door, open or otherwise, and the gulf between the haves and have-nots grows larger.

Access must mean more than an open door. It must also mean removing barriers to participation. Colleges cannot shirk this challenge. They must assertively develop outreach activities that will meet the needs of all potential learners. Community colleges that truly want to serve their communities must seek out those individuals who would benefit from program offerings but who, for any number of cultural or economic reasons, have not approached the open door on their own. The vitality of a community depends on this broader view of access.

INCLUSIVENESS

Inclusive community colleges strive to create positive environments for all people, regardless of gender, age, race, ethnicity, religion, disability, class, or sexual orientation. They develop organizational climates that allow learners and college personnel to communicate positively with each other. They also encourage collegewide participation in programs and activities. Community colleges have an excellent record of welcoming individuals from minority groups, and minority students have responded enthusiastically by enrolling at increasing rates. For example, although they make up less than 40 percent of all higher education institutions in the nation, community colleges teach:

- 46 percent of all African American college students
- 55 percent of all Hispanic college students
- 46 percent of all Asian and Pacific Islander college students
- 55 percent of all Native American college students
- 47 percent of all college students with disabilities
- 44 percent of all single-parent college students
- 50 percent of all college students over the age of 30
- 46 percent of all college students who work at least part time
- 50 percent of all first-generation college students

Community colleges have a right to be proud of their record of attracting underrepresented groups to higher education, but still not enough enrolled minority students earn certificates or degrees. This must change. So-called minorities will soon be the majority population in many urban areas and states. They value the ability to participate fully in the economy, and their participation influences the success of their families, their communities, and the nation. Community colleges must help more students from ethnic and other minority groups complete their educational goals. Colleges that develop a healthy, inclusive campus climate, along with strategies to support student learning,

RECOMMENDATIONS

- Community colleges should embrace "learning" rather than "teaching" as the focus of their educational enterprise and should focus on how different learning styles affect outcomes.

- Community colleges should take proactive measures to ensure that all community members have the necessary incentives, support, and opportunity to meet their education and training goals.

- Community colleges must welcome and support all people regardless of age, gender, race, ethnicity, religion, class, disability, sexual orientation, or other factors.

- Community colleges should develop strategies for maintaining a gender balance in enrollment and staffing.

- Community colleges must aggressively implement strategies to create campus climates that promote inclusiveness as an institutional and community value.

have a better chance of increasing student persistence than colleges that do not make this effort.

Community colleges should look closely at campus climate. Each institution should review its institutional mission statement. Does the statement encourage diversity?

Inclusion. North Seattle Community College set new multicultural requirements for associate degrees, including understanding ethnic and cultural differences in the United States. An advisory committee monitors the effects of the new curriculum on campus climate.

Does it stimulate an academic environment that engenders healthy race and ethnic relations—in fact, healthy relations among all groups? Surveys of learners, faculty, and staff can gauge the campus climate and the reality of the college mission. The information gleaned in this process can suggest ways to address those various relationships, including learner-faculty and faculty-administrator relationships. The goal is not for community colleges to be homogeneous places, nor to be merely tolerant ones, but to be places of understanding where differences are valued and respected.

The absence of men on college campuses, especially minority males, is emerging as a serious national concern. While women began to level the playing field over the last decades, men have absented themselves from higher education in growing numbers. Colleges must persist in eliminating glass ceilings for women, but they and the nation cannot afford to ignore the loss of men, especially minority men, in higher education. Although the reason for the imbalance is not clear, the new gender-inequity situation raises serious concerns, from the social and economic well-being of families to questions about the impact on classroom climate, career choices, and civic participation. As community colleges develop strategies for diverse and inclusive bodies of learners, faculty, administrators, and trustees, they must consider gender balance.

CURRICULUM

As the focus shifts from teaching to learning, the role of curriculum increases in importance. Each learner must understand completely the course goals, expected skills or knowledge to be acquired, and course content and sequencing necessary to achieve the goals. Doing all this in an organized fashion is the process of curriculum construction—a process that community colleges should execute more skillfully. Curricular planning must include conversations about the role of general education in community colleges as well as the impact on community colleges of academic and occupational skill standards, high-school programs, and the increasing interest in baccalaureate programming.

The Associate Degree

Community colleges affirm the associate degree as central to their mission. The associate degree establishes the community college vision of what it means to be an educated person for faculty, administrators, students, and society. It sets academic standards and goals for student achievement. Not every person who enters a community college intends to earn a degree, but for those who aspire to one and achieve it, the associate degree represents an important symbol of accomplishment and a passport to employment or to upper division collegiate work.

General Education

The general education curriculum, in particular, requires a careful look. As the body of knowledge essential for an educated person, the general education curriculum should empower people to engage in contemporary issues, appreciate and contribute to their culture, and appreciate their heritage. Colleges must find ways to include opportunities for experiential learning, such as service learning, in all of their educational offerings.

Community colleges must produce the best-prepared students possible for transfer into four-year colleges and universities. Because the general education curriculum provides the background people need to help them adapt to change, it should be considered a dynamic, not static, collection of courses. In today's environment, for example, familiarity with information technology and the global community as well as American cultures is essential. Though no single algorithm holds the answer for determining the core curriculum, educators developing it must share a vision of its goals.

Curriculum Development

As more curricula become available through the Internet and elsewhere, and as the practice of sharing curricula among institutions continues to grow, colleges must develop strategies for coordinated approaches to curriculum construction. Curriculum designers can provide support for faculty creating a new curriculum or revising an existing one. All faculty should teach from up-to-date materials. Although limited financial resources may restrict what some community colleges can support, they should do everything possible to ensure strong curricula and high-quality instructional materials. Curriculum revisions should reflect strategies for active, participatory learning for all.

Industry-Based Standards

The national demand for learning outcomes has prompted some colleges to evaluate student proficiencies according to industry-based skill standards. These credentials are gaining currency among employers because they report student skills more precisely than do traditional letter grades. Many underemployed degree holders suffer from the mismatch between what they learned and what they actually need to know for better jobs. As community colleges develop curricula

RECOMMENDATIONS

- Community colleges should review their vision of the role of general education and align their core courses with this vision.

- Community colleges should develop comprehensive strategies for providing an array of experiential learning opportunities, including service learning, that promote democratic skills along with academic and technical competence.

- Community colleges should make dynamic curriculum construction, management, and delivery processes, including collaborative arrangements, an institutional priority in planning and resource allocation.

- Community colleges should use recognized occupational skill standards in developing curriculum for occupational education and training.

- Community colleges must repackage their courses, policies, and schedules to meet the needs of lifelong learners as customers.

using occupational skill standards, the gap between learning outcomes and job requirements should diminish.

Industry skill standards. Bellevue Community College, Washington, and its Northwest Center for Emerging Technologies developed skill standards for information technology in conjunction with industry leaders. The Maricopa Advanced Technological Education Center in Arizona has done the same for semiconductor manufacturing.

The Secondary-Baccalaureate Squeeze

Educators and policymakers in and around community colleges are looking for ways to ease educational transitions from high school to universities. Partnerships with secondary schools that allow high school students to receive dual high school and college credit for courses are moving, in some cases, toward agreements for massive concurrent-enrollment programs. Collaboration between community colleges and universities in some communities allows students to take upper-level courses at or near the community college. Other community colleges offer courses for baccalaureate credit or require a bachelor's degree for entry into an associate degree program. Still others become four-year colleges. All of these connections are fascinating, but they may come with some risk. Community colleges and state systems considering implementation strategies for these transitions should look carefully at possible long-term effects. Will high school–community college–university curricular lines blur? Will the associate degree maintain its value as a credential? Can community colleges retain their identity and mission?

TECHNOLOGY

The widespread use of technology is transforming the learning process. Many people's learning time does not conform to daytime or early evening hours. Web-based courses and other distance-learning options facilitate asynchronous learning at the time and place of a student's choosing. College instruction no longer relies entirely on gatherings in a lecture hall or laboratory where a teacher distributes information in structured formats and prescribed timelines. Technology does not replace faculty, but it changes the teacher-learner relationship. Technology compels learners to be more active participants in the learning process. This shift means that instructors become facilitators, strategists, and coordinators for learning rather than lecturers or assigners of lessons and homework. They must focus more on different learning styles, conditions for learning, appropriate climate, goals, content, sequencing, and a multitude of strategies for optimal learning experiences.

Accepting these restructuring changes and adjusting to them is a challenge for faculty and administrators. Faculty should not be disheartened or threatened. Technology is a teaching and learning tool, not a substitute for excellent teaching. Community college faculty—by virtue of their education, expertise, and experience—have much to offer learners. As teachers and mentors, faculty understand different learning styles, support and direct learners' personal goals, and help establish paths to reach them.

SUPPORT SERVICES

Learner Support

Learners need a support system that helps them succeed. Unfortunately, student services often are the first hit and the last to recover from budget cuts. Years of tight finances mean many community colleges need to strengthen their learner-support systems. Colleges must discover more about their students, their aspirations, and their opinions of their college experiences in order to respond fully to learners' needs.

Many community colleges continue to structure their services and support systems around recent high school graduates, even though the average age of enrollees is 30. The conventional model of student services is built more for the convenience of the staff than for the people who form the majority of the learner population. Many people enrolled in community colleges are the first in their families or the first among their friends to attend college. They face unfamiliar routines on campus. The hectic pace of most community college students' days—a busy combination of work, class, and home responsibilities—leaves little time for the informal conversations that help students navigate an institution.

Community colleges can improve connections with their learners in a variety of ways. Ideally, all community college students should begin their academic careers with a one-on-one conversation with a faculty or staff member who can help them map an academic plan based on personal goals. Effective use of technology can facilitate interaction between students and academic advisers and follow-up on individual progress after students leave the college.

Transitional learners probably need more substantial services, such as special assessments, frequent adviser contact, test-taking clinics, remedial courses, and English-as-a-second-language courses. Additional support services such as childcare and transportation can make the difference between a student's completing a program or dropping out of it.

> *"America has a great advantage over other countries—our commitment to fully develop the talents of all of our citizens. Community colleges play a key role. We know that our country has no one to waste."*
> *—Robert McCabe*

RECOMMENDATIONS

■ Community colleges should develop policies to ensure excellence and appropriateness in high school concurrent-enrollment programs.

■ Community colleges that offer bachelor's degrees should maintain their identity and integrity as community-based institutions.

■ Community colleges must help faculty understand and integrate technology as an essential learning tool.

■ Each community college should ensure that its learner support systems provide attentive advising, services, and follow-up for all students.

■ Community colleges must embrace remedial education as an access point to higher education and increased opportunity and must make remedial courses mandatory for all learners who need them.

■ Community colleges should give reentry and disadvantaged learners, including those in remedial programs, the same priority and support as all other learners.

Remedial Education
Learners who, for a number of reasons, are not prepared for college-level work often face a difficult transition into college. One of the first responsibilities of a community college is to provide another chance for such learners. It opens doors of opportunity for recent high school graduates, adults long out of school with new educational aspirations, and immigrants of all ages striving for success in a new country. Remedial education represents a key part of the access puzzle and must be an important activity of any community college. It must remain so as long as the need for it exists.

Retaining students. The Community College of Denver has a decade-long commitment to student success. Strategies include competency-based courses, reading and writing labs, course evaluations, and a strong student support system. Student performance and satisfaction with faculty are consistently high.

Remediation is not an excuse to lower the bar in terms of graduation or certification requirements or grades. The worth of any educational experience lies in the value it adds to a person's life. Preparing a remedial student to do college work successfully is as laudable and worthy as seeing a baccalaureate graduate admitted to a first-rate doctoral program. Those who advocate the elimination of remedial education are wrong. Until all learners come fully prepared for academic work, community colleges have an obligation to offer high-quality remedial courses that will help learners succeed. Efforts to improve the prospects of remedial-education students should begin by making remediation courses mandatory for all who need them.

CREDENTIALING

As governments and employers demand evidence of learning, the inadequacy of traditional college transcripts has become more obvious. Different courses may look the same on a transcript. The transcript reflects neither course objectives nor skills acquired. Business leaders have little confidence in letter grades as accurate measures of knowledge or skill. Increasingly mobile workers need portable credentials that explicitly document what they can do. The traditional academic-accounting system does not reflect the multiplicity of educational sources used by most learners. Learning occurs not only in classrooms but also on the job, in meetings, through travel and reading, and in self-paced independent studies. People acquire knowledge and skills in many ways, such as internships, field experience, community leadership, volunteerism, and service learning. Traditional benchmarks like degrees and certificates do not capture or reflect the value of these varied experiences.

Despite these inadequacies, degrees and certificates continue to play a strong role as passports to social status and admittance to four-year institutions. This dichotomy raises crucial questions about the best method for assessing and recording learning. Community colleges may help resolve this dilemma by creating centers for coordinating and conducting learning assessments. The colleges could provide career transcripts of adult experiential learning in addition to traditional academic transcripts.

LIFELONG LEARNING

Learning over a lifetime is essential for everyone—children, parents, seniors. One of the vast opportunities for the community college is to lead the community in lifelong learning. This effort has

Documenting skills. The SCANS 2000 Center is working on projects that will create a Career Transcript System. Chandler-Gilbert Community College, Arizona, Hocking Technical College, Ohio, and Monroe Community College, New York, document a student's service learning experience on academic transcripts.

immense implications for establishing partnerships and for dealing with community problems. By their outreach efforts, community colleges have redefined learners to include those who avail themselves of the programs, services, and facilities open to the public, not just to people paying tuition to take courses. Changing societal and economic conditions in recent years have reinforced the idea that people at every stage of life benefit from formal as well as informal learning.

The idea of lifelong learning—that one could take college courses beyond the "traditional" 18-to-22 college age—was a community college initiative from the beginning. Its widespread acceptance is one of the most important outcomes of the community college movement. Change is constant and so must be learning. Today's workers must continually upgrade their skills and knowledge to stay employable. Some experts predict that future workers will devote a portion of every day to learning at the workplace.

RECOMMENDATIONS

- Community colleges should identify alternative approaches that augment conventional academic transcripts to communicate fully a learner's skills, knowledge, and relevant experience to prospective employers or other educational institutions.

- Community colleges should analyze the learning assessment process and become centers for the assessment of specific skills required by employers.

- Community colleges should provide strategies for lifelong learning and develop programs for every age level.

- Community college personnel must be appropriately informed about the various federal, state, and other assistance programs available to support lifelong learners.

- Community colleges must adopt strategies to alert graduates, other students, and community members to new learning opportunities and to financial assistance sources available to lifelong learners.

CHAPTER 3

College Connections

To create a learning-centered environment that will lead people to the knowledge net, all members of the college community must be partners for student success. A productive partnership will allow administrators, faculty, labor unions, trustees, and others to place learning and student success as the institution's highest priorities.

HUMAN RESOURCES

Without attention to personnel contributions and needs, an institution has little chance of remaining current or flexible enough to meet public demands successfully. All personnel must demonstrate an ability and a willingness to perform their duties, adapt to change, understand the college mission, and carry out the college's commitments to community service. Their actions should reflect respect for the contributions of every

sector of the community and for the needs of the individuals and groups encountered.

Faculty

Community college leaders would do well to examine the gulfs that exist among faculty and staff and should seek remedies. The distance that sometimes exists between full-time and adjunct faculty is one example of counterproductive fragmentation. Compelling financial and pedagogical reasons lead to the hiring of adjuncts. Other personnel do not always consider adjuncts to be full-fledged members of the academic community—even when they outnumber other instructional staff. Esteem for full-time faculty and collegial relations with adjuncts should not be mutually exclusive. Bringing adjuncts into the fold of the colleges will serve learners better.

In many community colleges, a disparity exists between the percentages of students and faculty from minority groups. The diversity of faculty and staff says a great deal about an institution's commitment to diversity, and efforts should be made to honor that commitment. In homogeneous communities, faculty and staff from diverse backgrounds can help open eyes to differences and allow learners to see worlds and viewpoints beyond their own. Homogeneous communities that seek and hire these faculty and staff must do everything possible to make the environment a welcoming one.

Community colleges may find it helpful to work with universities and businesses to strengthen the pipeline for community college faculty and to attract new people to the profession. Community colleges should seek to collaborate with businesses to create incentives, such as scholarships, for graduate students who

RECOMMENDATIONS

■ Community colleges must create a positive, professional work environment that values all personnel regardless of classification.

■ Community colleges should seek and hire diverse and competent faculty and staff in every part of the institution.

■ Community colleges should allocate at least 2 percent of their annual operating budgets to the professional development and training of their personnel.

■ Community colleges must prepare more people for higher education leadership roles and strive for more diversity in all leadership positions.

■ Universities should initiate or strengthen leadership programs that will prepare a new generation of community college leaders.

■ Community colleges should recognize the importance of physical and mental health in the learning, retention, productivity, and well-being of all persons, and should respond with programming, policies, and services to promote a healthful environment for learning.

Recruiting new faculty. Santa Fe (Florida) Community College provides a $9,000 stipend to selected minority students in University of Florida doctoral programs. In exchange, the graduate students agree to help recruit and keep minority students at Santa Fe and to teach three courses a year there during their university study. Santa Fe offers them full-time employment upon graduation.

commit to teaching in community colleges. A college and a business might agree to share a particularly skilled faculty member's compensation expenses, so instructors in high-demand fields would find it feasible to dedicate some of their time to teaching. Colleges might also address competitive demands for instructor skills by adopting compensatory systems based on market demand and performance merit.

Professional Development
Professional development—lifelong learning—is as important for community college personnel as it is for students and other workers. It can help keep an institution viable, especially as colleges adopt new technologies to provide courses, programs, and services. Colleges should think creatively. Faculty externships or special projects can energize even long-term faculty. Colleges must devote sufficient funds to faculty and staff development. The amount will vary from one institution to another, but a reasonable start would be 2 percent of the operating budget. The American Association of Community Colleges and Association of Community College Trustees have suggested this benchmark in the past

and for several years their members have debated its merits.

Developing Leaders

Community colleges across the nation face a leadership crisis and an unparalleled opportunity to meet that crisis. They must build a new leadership pipeline. As senior administrators and faculty retire in record numbers, the leadership of many institutions is being passed to a new generation. Many of those retiring have worked in community colleges since the 1960s, when hundreds of new colleges opened. These leadership transitions provide an opportunity for community colleges to create professional staffs with more diversity. Although community college enrollments generally reflect the racial and ethnic diversity of their communities, the faculty and administration at most community colleges have been composed largely of nonminority persons. Identifying and preparing more women and people from underrepresented groups to fill community college presidencies and upper-level administrative slots is essential.

With the large number of anticipated retirements, community colleges must make a greater effort to prepare people for the rigors of college leadership. In addition to encouraging colleagues to acquire graduate degrees—the traditional approach—top administrators can look at other avenues, such as fellowship programs or leadership institutes, to draw new candidates. Mentoring younger staff is another approach. Many college-management skills—negotiating, fundraising, policymaking, and lobbying—can be learned on the job under the tutelage of an experienced guide before one becomes a college president. More universities should initiate leadership programs for community college administrators. Such programs played an invaluable role in preparing leaders from the 1960s to the 1990s.

Health and Wellness

Every institution's agenda must include attention to the physical, mental, and environmental well-being of all students and college personnel. Issues may vary from college to college, but the outcome is similar. In any community, physically and emotionally unwell people do not learn or contribute to their fullest and may cause harm to others. Thoughtful

New leaders. The Kentucky Leadership Academy trains new leaders through an annual professional development and mentoring program for faculty and administrators in the state's community and technical colleges. Iowa State University runs a program with similar goals for the state's community college faculty and administrators. Both aim to bring more women and minorities into leadership positions.

Health and wellness. St. Louis Community College's mission statement promises an environment that fosters the well-being of everyone it serves. An Iowa Lakes Community College partnership with the community built a popular swimming center on the college campus. At Rio Hondo (California) College's fitness center, an unusual dress code encourages loose-fitting clothing and sets a welcoming atmosphere for out-of-shape exercisers. Raritan Valley Community College, New Jersey, provides regular HIV testing on campus.

curricular, service, and policy strategies can help create healthier campuses. Health information is a common part of the curriculum for allied health occupations, but colleges can incorporate it into general education courses. Information on epidemiology, emotional counseling, homeopathic remedies, or HIV prevention are just a few examples. Policies regarding smoking, alcohol use, and substance abuse can help community colleges promote good health habits. College decisions on policies regarding family leave, reproductive-health services, referrals for services, and fitness programs influence the actions of others within the community.

TECHNOLOGY

Technology does not work efficiently without human input. Community colleges must develop and maintain technology-planning processes that include all sectors of the college community, including the faculty, and all areas of the campus for which information technology is used—telephone and library services, administrative services, academic computing, networking, and so on. The technology plan should meet the latest accessibility standards for persons with disabilities.

The rapid pace of innovation and the unpredictability about how the general public will use innovations complicate the creation of a college's strategic plan for technology. In less than a decade, the Internet grew from a small system for researchers into a worldwide system for mass communication and commerce. An institutional technology plan must set goals yet must be flexible on the details for achieving these goals, because innova-

tions cause continual change. For instance, computers for all full-time faculty and staff or a campus computer system that can be accessed off campus are technology goals that would be revised as equipment changes.

A campuswide technology plan should address and integrate the administrative, academic, and student needs of the college. Planners need to consider the match between on-campus services and services available online. Must online students come to campus to get counseling or buy books? Successfully integrating technology into all aspects of college operations takes a great deal of work and requires commitment and support from college leaders.

Technology, as a tool, helps colleges achieve their missions. It should neither set the agenda nor drive the strategic plan. Those working on a technology plan should consider their college's overall mission in establishing technological goals, assessing existing technologies, and then examining the gap between those technologies and the college's ultimate goals.

Technology should be considered a permanent part of community college budgets, not an addendum. It is not a one-time expense but an investment. There is no way to avoid periodic updating of computer hardware and software even when equipment-recycling programs are in place. Colleges must temper their enthusiasm for technology and the desire to have the latest, fastest models with evaluations of how new equipment fits institutional goals and existing capacity. Novice planners should be careful about jumping into complicated systems too quickly.

Those working on technology plans must be realistic about the effect of technology on college personnel. In most instances, especially when faculty and staff

Institutional technology plans. A college's mission—to provide accessible, high-quality education for its often-diverse community—lies at the heart of its technology plan. St. Louis Community College's plan addresses technology infrastructure, student learning, and administrative efficiency. The plan at Community College of Allegheny County, Pennsylvania, acknowledges rapid change and commits to continuous evaluation of new technology and applications and to raising its county's quality of life.

begin their learning, technology takes more time, not less. Just corresponding with students by e-mail takes time. Technology has the potential to customize instruction to accommodate differences in students' preparation, learning styles, schedules, and goals. But this fluency does not happen automatically; it takes time and practice. To incorporate technology fully, faculty, staff, and learners need up-front training and ongoing support.

Tech-savvy faculty and staff. Institutions take various paths to help faculty stay up-to-date in their technology skills. Information technology faculty and staff at Aims Community College, Colorado, teach non-IT faculty how to move their courses online. Cerritos College, California, provides training to faculty and staff through its Innovation Center. IT students help faculty develop Web pages at Camden County College, New Jersey.

RECOMMENDATIONS

- Community colleges must seek bold and unconventional approaches and consult with all stakeholders when developing information technology plans.
- Community colleges must plan for technological upgrading as a routine part of budgeting and resource allocation.
- Computer literacy must be a core requirement for all community college students and faculty.
- Community colleges must develop adequate online support services for students and faculty to accompany online curricula.
- Community colleges must make the online environment accessible to all students and community members.
- The quality of all electronic courses and services must be equal to or better than those on campus.

The use of computer technology across the curriculum should be mandatory, with computer-literacy requirements for all degrees and certificates. Even as people use computer technology for different purposes across careers—art history research, tax preparation, automobile repair, food service, banking, nursing, farming—colleges must integrate technology into the curriculum in such a way that students can enter their chosen careers with confidence.

The digital divide remains a serious concern for community colleges. Technology is becoming yet another wedge between the haves and have-nots of every community. Community colleges need to guard against leaving behind people who cannot afford their own computers. Generously equipped and adequately staffed computer labs with long hours are a must. Colleges also should explore ways of giving or lending equipment to students from disadvantaged households and should work with libraries and others to develop resource networks.

Community colleges should not use technology to skimp or cut corners. The Internet expands the offerings of campus libraries, but it does not replace them. It provides accessibility for specialized programs to students who attend rural or small colleges, but only if they have the academic foundation and the technology to access the programs. Although technology can enhance the intellectual give-and-take between instructors and students, it does not eliminate the need for faculty. Colleges may save money by using already-established electronic courses, but they should not resort to perpetuating outdated materials or lectures just to reduce expenses. Technology should provide a way of making the learning process better, not just a different method of doing the same things.

Colleges must not see electronic education as a means of abandoning their commitment to hard-to-serve students. All students—even those with disabilities or a need for remedial or English-as-a-second-language instruction—should have access to electronic courses. Standards must remain high for electronic courses so that there is no question about course quality. Although many faculty and students find technology fun, that characteristic should not define an electronic course. Besides making these online courses available to all learners, colleges should provide online-support services. Faculty require support and training, and students need services equal to those offered on campus, such as study groups, library resources, and advisement. All groups need easily accessible technical support.

ACCREDITATION

Accountability demands an assurance of institutional and program quality. Quality assurance also builds trust and credibility with the service community as well as other members of the higher education community. The principal tool is accreditation. For institutional assurance, regional accreditation is the tool of choice; for program-quality assurance, specialized accreditation serves the same purpose. In recent years, regional accrediting agencies have moved toward student-performance standards in an attempt to shore up their role as gatekeepers for institutional eligibility for certain federal programs. This trend demonstrates how closely quality assurance is connected with accountability.

Although technically a voluntary process, quality assurance through accreditation is a de facto mandatory process that can be expensive and time consuming. Community college administrators should view the accreditation process as a planning tool.

GOVERNING THE CONNECTED COLLEGE

The essence of the community college lies in its community-based nature. As a voice for the community, the board of trustees ensures that the college serves the community's interest. Community college success arises from this unity of purpose. To avoid becoming insular, self-serving, and eventually irrelevant, community colleges must maintain this strong community connection, and boards must connect as closely as possible to the community. Community-based trustees most likely can best understand the community's needs and ensure that the college meets them. State boards can meet this challenge by using local advisory boards.

Communities do not function in isolation, even when the state governance structure includes local governing boards. Because economic and workforce development and overall quality-of-life issues do not adhere to legally defined community or college service-area boundaries, statewide coordination is necessary. Since the state's interest flows from its many communities, the statewide governance structure should be a confederation of local college-community interests.

Election and appointment processes both work well in trustee selection, but effective boards require the continuing participation of community leaders. Local boards and state and national trustee associations must communicate the characteristics that define effective trusteeship. To work well in the complex, fast-paced, and politically charged arena of public higher education, good governance relies on a clear understanding of the board's role, which must be specified in board policy, statute, or regulation.

Board members must recognize their role as an independent community voice that is most effective and that serves community interests best when their actions satisfy all participants. Board policy must ensure that all trustees and staff members respect the president as the link between the board and students, faculty, and staff. Board members should not use their personal expertise to manage the college. Trustees who do so violate the role differentiation between themselves and the college's chief executive officer.

Development of an effective board-CEO team begins with a participatory and inclusive CEO-selection process. Board policies provide direction for

RECOMMENDATIONS

- Community colleges should ensure that the accrediting process meets their quality assurance and public accountability goals and use it for strategic planning and professional development.

- State systems must recognize and respect the role of locally connected governing boards in representing community and college interests.

- Governing boards must communicate the characteristics of effective trusteeship and cultivate future trustees who exhibit those qualities.

- Governing boards must define their roles clearly and commit to represent the interests of the community.

- Trustees and the college's chief executive officer must act as a leadership team and respect their differing leadership roles.

- Trustees should participate in local, state, and national in-service training.

expected institutional outcomes and the ethical context in which they are to be pursued. Governing boards provide CEOs with a supportive working environment, appropriate compensation package, and guidelines for evaluation.

Boards must adopt, follow, and enforce standards of conduct that respect the public trust. Trustees have a responsibility to pursue the community's best interest, regardless of their own points of view or those of a particular interest group. Once the board has made a decision, trustees should cease debate and support the decision. They must understand that it is the board, not the individual trustee members, that has authority. Trustees conduct their affairs

Training new trustees. Trustee education is so important that some states have put it into law. A 1999 North Carolina statute allows a board of trustees to declare vacant the position of a trustee who, without justifiable excuse, does not participate in a state association-sponsored trustee orientation and education session within six months of appointment.

with the knowledge that their actions affect the image, and value, of the college held by its students, faculty and staff, the public, legislators, and accrediting bodies.

The complexity of discharging the responsibility of a trustee today is staggering. It requires a firm grasp of the role and process of governance and a continually updated understanding of the social, economic, political, and educational environment in which a college operates. Effective governance requires that trustees design and participate in their own professional-development experiences locally and through their state and national organizations.

FINANCE

Resources

Although community colleges are well positioned as important and valued institutions, their accomplishments often can be attributed more to the extraordinary effort and dedication of trustees, faculty, and staff than to the skillful allocation of financial resources. Typically, scarce financial resources challenge community colleges to do more with less than in

any other segment of education. Some might view this as clever and efficient. Over time, however, it has the potential of backfiring and causing a significant loss of effectiveness. This pitfall must be avoided.

Communities and those empowered to allocate resources must nurture their community colleges. Well-tended colleges have adequate financial resources; sufficient faculty, professional staff, and support staff; sufficient technological and other equipment; a suitable complex of physical facilities; and a reasonable capacity to sustain and maintain the college. Money makes it possible for community colleges to serve their communities and learners. While generally received from state, federal, local, private, and learner sources, funding varies from state to state. One state channels funds through county boards, while another levies taxes. Average in-state annual tuition ranges from a few hundred dollars in some states to a few thousand dollars in others. With such differences, it is not practical to focus on all the variables of funding for each community college in the United States.

Instead, it is important to focus on one common financial issue. Every state uses some form of learner "seat time" to determine the level of appropriations.

Funding support. Maryland funds noncredit instruction—including any contract training but no recreational activities—at the same level as credit instruction. Through a performance contract with the state board of regents, each Ohio campus receives $50,000 to support training and assessment services to Ohio employers and is then eligible for additional funds based upon the level of services provided.

College leaders have long viewed this practice as a barrier to serving their communities fully because it does not address noninstructional community issues or provide services to youths or older adults. It also generally does not support workplace training. In spite of some attempts, a more flexible approach has not been developed satisfactorily.

Some state governments are pushing performance-based funding. Most states that have used it have decided to allocate a portion of their funds based on performance criteria adopted by the state's legislature. On its face, performance-based funding has the potential to resolve some of the negative features of credit hour–driven funding. Reporting educational outcomes by the number of students who attained their personal goals, passed licensing exams, or found work in their field of study does have the advantage of publicizing a wider range of activities than do graduation and transfer rates.

The motives behind performance-based funding, however, can be problematic and even constraining. If states adopt the performance-based approach to fund the community services a college provides, it would help address the unmet financial needs of community colleges. But if the rationale is merely to save money and demand more accountability, it will not do so.

Disconnects

The divergence between the political reality of the appropriations process and the strong service culture that defines community colleges represents another funding challenge. The rigid funding process does not respond with sensitivity to large deviations from the historical norm or recent past practices.

Consider what would usually happen if a state system of community colleges

RECOMMENDATIONS

■ Community college leaders should advocate for funding flexibility to support expanding programs that are not based solely on full-time-equivalent criteria.

■ By using a strategic approach and seeking political allies who share common goals, community colleges must aggressively make their case for greater funding to accommodate increased enrollment and service needs.

experienced a 20 percent increase in enrollment during the year in which the appropriation was based. If this happened, it is highly unlikely that the system would realize a 20 percent increase in funds. The reason is that community college budgets are tied to other, unrelated sectors of the state budget. If a state's revenue and the cost of doing business increase at a rate of 4 percent, most state agencies would get just a 4 percent increase. The hypothesized 20 percent enrollment growth could be accommodated only at the expense of other agencies or educational institutions. It can easily be seen that a challenging political situation results and that large increases in appropriations will be difficult, though not impossible, to achieve.

Tribal colleges, which get most of their funds from the federal government, face a particularly poignant situation. They must compete with other American Indian education and healthcare programs. Most of these colleges receive the majority of their operating and capital funds through the Tribally Controlled College or University Assistance Act, which Congress has never funded at the authorized levels. The colleges get little state funding because they lie on federal trust lands, and local property taxes cannot be levied on trust lands. A few tribal colleges get a share of the profits from the casinos and other enterprises located on trust lands, but the amount they receive is relatively small and unpredictable. Most tribal colleges survive by cobbling together grants with tuition fees, which are high in comparison to the poverty of their students. With rapidly growing populations, these colleges confront a special challenge in serving their communities.

Rural community colleges in general have special circumstances that warrant consideration for extra funding. About one-third of the nation's community colleges are located in rural areas or in towns with fewer than 25,000 residents. In many of these places, community colleges are the centers of the community. As more people leave rural areas, the colleges must contend with a scarcity of financial and human resources. Usually small institutions, they generally have large service areas. They lack the economies of scale enjoyed by larger urban and suburban institutions and as a result have higher per-student costs. On top of these financial challenges, many rural colleges struggle with out-migration and the loss of intellectual capital—brain drain—when graduates leave the region for employment. Rural community colleges also have difficulty attracting faculty and staff because they cannot offer the salaries and amenities available in suburban and urban areas.

Nationally, high school graduation rates and immigration will create a surge in community college enrollments, particularly in high-growth states. This comes at a time when the best financial predictions lead to the conclusion that existing revenue structures cannot maintain current levels of services. This collision of insufficient revenue and increased demand presents higher education leaders with the unpleasant choice of increasing student fees or reducing costs or a combination of both. Undesirable fee increases yield only limited gains because a larger proportion of fees must be allocated as financial aid for other students. An economic downturn will make matters worse.

A final comment on funding relates to the long-standing feeling that community colleges are poorly funded when compared with universities. Equitable funding—equal appropriations for educating freshmen and sophomores throughout a state's higher education system—would be the optimal way of resolving community colleges' financial problems. Until that ideal is achieved, it is in the best interest of community colleges to make a case for funding based on financial needs to support programs and services. Community colleges have a compelling story to tell, and the more effectively it is told with solid data, the closer they will come to resolving their financial needs.

CHAPTER 4

The Challenge

The Knowledge Net intends to create a common vision and roadmap for America's community colleges for the first decade of the 21st century. This report, of necessity, rests heavily on the past and present. Although the future is difficult to predict, some things are certain. Change, driven by accelerating technological development, will be pervasive. Market demands for timely, competitive services will accelerate, as will demands for accountability at all levels. The community college mission appears to be in flux. The global marketplace will require colleges to produce learners with new competencies at the same time that institutions face a staffing crisis. The educational community will face continued pressure to keep up with constant change.

Fiber-optic systems, computers, digitization, wireless communication, and the Internet—though still in their infancies—will affect education and train-

ing enterprises indefinitely. It is not practical to make specific predictions about applications of these technologies, but it is feasible to emphasize in no uncertain terms that community colleges must stay alert and informed by subscribing to cutting-edge periodicals, attending forward-thinking conferences, and building staff expertise. Without doubt, colleges must create institutional climates that encourage experimentation and risk-taking and engage staff at all levels.

Community colleges must find strategies for staying responsive to community needs as the pace of change quickens. Customers and learners will demand more timely programs and services, and these will be delivered in an increasingly competitive environment. Community colleges may have to choose between general or specialized programs and services. They face hurdles caused by regulatory requirements and restrictions on revenue creation. Much is riding on how community colleges meet these challenges.

Public and governmental demands for accountability continue to grow. The trend is rooted in decreasing confidence in public institutions, in changing priorities for allocating funds, and in the growing national importance of education and training. Community colleges have little choice but to expend more funds for tracking those who graduate as well as those who leave, to collect more data, and to conduct more research. These follow-up efforts must be done in a way that does not diminish the college's capacity to serve, respond, and adapt.

The mission of community colleges has changed substantially since they were founded a century ago, and change continues. In order to serve their communities more fully, some community colleges are awarding the "applied" or even the traditional baccalaureate degree. Florida has already granted baccalaureate authority to all its community colleges under certain conditions. For now, these baccalaureate-granting institutions pledge to remain classified as community colleges. At the same time, half of the nation's state colleges and universities offer the associate degree. The lines are blurring.

Concurrent (dual or joint) enrollments represent a stronger trend. The practice of simultaneously granting high school credit and college credit to students enrolled in regular community college courses is gaining strength. The governor of Utah wants every student to graduate from high school with an associate degree—a bold vision that stands the traditional community college mission on its ear. Two of the state's community colleges already offer a bachelor's degree, and a third is not far behind. This squeeze leaves community colleges on the margin of what has been mainstream for most of the 20th century. Mission blur is happening at both the secondary–community college and the community

college–university junctures. The three-year baccalaureate is another example, and others will surface in coming years. Together, they will have a dramatic impact on community colleges as we now know them and may redefine how the colleges respond to change, to community needs, and to institutional staffing practices.

The next decade will see an immense growth in the need for global competence. Advancements in communication and transportation will shrink the distance between nations. The past several years have seen more businesses expand into the global economy to avoid shrinkage or closure. Employers deliberately may seek workers who have any kind of international experience. Community colleges must be ready to meet the needs of these companies and workers.

A huge restaffing effort is just around the corner. A serious talent war lurks, driven by simultaneous planned retirements and an economic expansion that requires educated workers for continued growth. Colleges will find themselves in the difficult position of needing to replace more faculty and staff than previously expected while maintaining personnel diversity. Institutional professional development programs must prepare new people to work effectively in community colleges. Large turnover rates will sorely test the ability of community colleges to maintain the character that has been shaped by a century of shared values, beliefs, and visions.

In the midst of all these economic, technological, and institutional changes, community colleges cannot afford to lose sight of the heart and soul of their identity—a close and consciously nurtured reflection of their communities. "Building communities" is more than a catch phrase; it is what community colleges are about. Societal change is accelerating alongside technological changes. People in neighborhoods as well as workplaces need communication and learning skills over a lifetime to direct change and to accommodate to it, and learner-centered community colleges hold the key to managing change and sustaining healthy communities. No other institution is situated more favorably than the community college to help bring about necessary changes in knowledge, skills, perspectives, attitudes, and values.

Current educational systems do not match today's reality. Education needs fundamental reform, but experience has shown that top-down efforts are not necessarily the answer. Community colleges—broadly based and interwoven with community networks—have the opportunity and the obligation to lead transformation that will meet the requirements of a citizenry engaged in lifelong learning. They must make serious connections, not just token gestures, with people and organizations working with early childhood education, elementary and secondary schools, and adult education in schools and the workplace. They must be prepared to serve the growing numbers of senior citizens seeking courses and training.

Community colleges must not only facilitate communication and learning but also must lead the changes needed for true lifelong learning in a world driven by technology and a global economy. At the same time that the Internet has become a household word, inspiring

images of one homogeneous worldwide community, the planet is in fact more fragmented. The search for identity, personal or national, threatens the common good, and human influences at all levels shape the mammoth changes set in motion by technology and globalization.

In spite of other demands on them, community colleges must continue to stretch to see the bigger picture around them. They must find answers to tough questions, even those that seem peripheral to education: Why does the nation spend more money on prisons than on schools? What drives some youth toward gangs and some adults toward hate groups? What kind of age discrimination will surface as elderly people outnumber workers? How can it be easy to ignore cries for qualified daycare providers while being horrified about child neglect? How will colleges assess these issues and stake a claim in the future?

Community colleges must prepare people to live in and to contribute to this new century. They must guide the development of technologically competent people who will be sensitive to the impact of their actions in the workplace, the community, and the world. They must produce people with occupational skills who also can think critically, solve problems, work and live ethically, and contribute to a democracy. Community colleges have demonstrated their capacity and commitment for 100 years. They now must sustain the climate of community that is their very essence and forge ahead to create new connections—human and electronic. They must proudly and purposefully assume their leadership position in the knowledge net.

Bibliography

AACC Policy Statement on the Associate Degree. 1999. Washington, D.C.: American Association of Community Colleges.

ACT. 1998. "Issues Confronting Community Colleges at the Onset of the 21st Century." Working paper, ACT, Iowa City, Iowa.

Adelman, Cliff. 1998. "What Proportion of College Students Earn a Degree?" *AAHE Bulletin* 51 (2): 7–9.

———. 1999a. *Answers in the Tool Box: Academic Intensity, Attendance Patterns, and Bachelor's Degree Attainment.* Jessup, Md.: U.S. Department of Education.

———. 1999b. Memorandum to New Expeditions Project, 5 May.

Aitken, Sally, et al. 1999. "Using Occupations to Improve Basic Skills: Integrating Occupational and Developmental Education." Forum at the 79th Annual Convention of American Association of Community Colleges, 9 April, Nashville.

Albright, Brenda Norman. 1997. "Of Carrots and State Budgets." *Trusteeship* 5 (March/April): 18–23.

———. 1998. *The Transition from Business as Usual to Funding for Results: State Efforts to Integrate Performance Measures in the Higher Education Budgetary Process.* Denver: State Higher Education Executive Officers. ERIC No. ED 418 652.

Alfred, Richard, and Patricia Carter. 2000. *Contradictory Colleges: Thriving in an Era of Continuous Change.* New Expeditions Issues Paper Series, no. 6. Washington, D.C.: Community College Press, American Association of Community Colleges.

Alfred, Richard, Peter Ewell, James Hudgins, and Kay McClenney. 1999. *Core Indicators of Effectiveness for Community Colleges.* 2d ed. Washington, D.C.: Community College Press, American Association of Community Colleges. ERIC No. ED 426 749.

American Association of University Women Educational Foundation. 1999. *Gaining a Foothold: Women's Transitions through Work and College.* Washington, D.C.: American Association of University Women Educational Foundation.

American Council on International Intercultural Education, Community Colleges for International Development, and The Stanley Foundation. 2000. *Charting the Future of Global Education in Community Colleges.* New Expeditions Issues Paper Series, no. 12. Washington, D.C.: Community College Press, American Association of Community Colleges.

American Indian Higher Education Consortium and the Institute for Higher Education Policy. 1999. *Tribal Colleges: An Introduction.* Alexandria, Va.: American Indian Higher Education Consortium.

Association of Governing Boards of Universities and Colleges. 1998. *AGB Statement on Institutional Governance.* Washington, D.C.: Association of Governing Boards of Universities and Colleges. ERIC No. ED 426 675.

Baker, George A., III. 1998. Memorandum to New Expeditions Project, 24 September.

———. 1999. Memorandum to New Expeditions Project, 17 February.

Barton, Thomas E., Jr. 1998. Letter to New Expeditions Project, 9 November.

Beheler, Ann. 1998. Interview by Madeline Patton, November.

Blandin Foundation. 1998a. *Addendum to Worker Education in Greater Minnesota: The Need for Life-Long Learning.* Grand Rapids, Minn.: Blandin Foundation.

———. 1998b. *Worker Education in Greater Minnesota: The Need for Life-Long Learning.* Grand Rapids, Minn.: Blandin Foundation.

Blevins, Vivian B. 1998. Letter to New Expeditions Project, 5 November.

Boggs, George R. 2000. "Community Colleges Have Key Teacher Training Role." *Community College Times* 25 January, 3, 9.

Bragg, Sadie C. 1998. *Investing in Tomorrow's Teachers: The Integral Role of Two-Year Colleges in the Science and Mathematics Preparation of Prospective Teacher.* Report from a National Science Foundation Workshop, March 12–14, 1998. Report NSF 99-49. Arlington, Va.: National Science Foundation. ERIC No. ED 427 968.

"Bringing Global Thinking to Community Colleges: International Program Director Strives to Reach Every Student." 1999. *Community College Times*, 9 March, 9.

Buettner, David L. 1999. Interview by Madeline Patton, May.

Burnham, Peter F. 1998. "Observations on Issues Affecting the Public Comprehensive Community College for the Next Decade." December. Typescript.

Calabro, Anthony D. 1998. Letter to New Expeditions Project, October.

California Citizens Commission on Higher Education. 1998. *A State of Learning: California Higher Education in the Twenty-First Century.* Los Angeles: California Citizens on Higher Education. ERIC No. ED 420 348.

Carnevale, Anthony P. 2000. Community *Colleges and Career Qualifications.* New Expeditions Issues Paper Series, no. 11. Washington, D.C.: Community College Press, American Association of Community Colleges.

Carnevale, Anthony P., Donna M. Desrochers, and Stephen J. Rose. 1998. "Community Colleges: A Vision Deferred." *Community College Journal* 68 (June/July): 26–33.

Christensen, Dennis, and Ray Taylor. 1999. "On the Effective Governance of Community Colleges." April. Typescript.

College of Lake County. 1997. *Preferred Futures @ CLC Report,* Grayslake, Ill.: College of Lake County.

Commission on the Future of Community Colleges. 1988. *Building Communities: A Vision for a New Century.* Washington, D.C.: American Association of Community Colleges. ERIC No. ED 293 578.

Copa, George H., and William Ammentorp. 1998. *New Designs for the Two-Year Institution of Higher Education: Final Report.* Berkeley, Calif.: National Center for Research in Vocational Education, University of California at Berkeley. ERIC No. ED 419 567.

Daggett, Willard R. 1998. Letter to New Expeditions Project, 7 July.

Davis, Bob, and David Wessel. 1999. *Prosperity: The Coming Twenty-Year Boom and What It Means to You.* New York: Random House.

Davis, Gary. *Issues in Community College Governance.* 2000. New Expeditions Issues Paper Series, no. 7. Washington, D.C.: Community College Press, American Association of Community Colleges.

Day, Larry L. 1998. *MS Public Community/Junior College Students Enrolled in MS Public Universities: An Initial Analysis.* Jackson, Miss.: Mississippi State Board for Community and Junior Colleges.

Delors, Jacques. 1996. *Learning: The Treasure Within.* Report to UNESCO of the International Commission on Education for the Twenty-First Century. Paris: UNESCO. ERIC No. ED 418 902.

Eaton, Judith S. 1998. Letter to New Expeditions Project, 29 September.

Edwards, Allen. 1998. "Issues for the Future." E-mail to New Expeditions Project, 30 October.

Eller, R., et al. 1999. *Rural Community College Initiative: IV. Capacity for Leading Institutional and Community Change.* Washington, D.C.: American Association of Community Colleges. ERIC No. ED 432 332.

ERIC Clearinghouse for Community Colleges. 1998. *New Expeditions—Vision and Direction for the Nation's Community Colleges.* Los Angeles: ERIC Clearinghouse for Community Colleges. ERIC No. ED 423 002.

Eskow, Seymour, and John Caffrey. 1974. "World Community College: A 20:20 Vision." *New Directions for Community Colleges* 7 (autumn): 71–80.

Eskow, Steve. 1998. "World Community College: Has Its Time Come?" San Francisco, 18 August. Typescript.

Fanelli, Sean A. 1998. Letter to New Expeditions Project, 5 August.

Ferguson, Richard L. 1998. Letter to New Expeditions Project, 27 October.

Flynn, William J. 2000. *The Search for the Learning-Centered College.* New Expeditions Issues Paper Series, no. 9. Washington, D.C.: Community College Press, American Association of Community Colleges.

Galston, William A., and Elaine C. Kamark. 1998. "Five Realities That Will Shape 21st-Century Politics." *Blueprint Magazine* (fall). Internet: http://www.dlc.org/blueprint/fall/98/article1.html [Accessed: 15 October 1998].

de la Garza, Leonardo. 1998. Letter to New Expeditions Project, 16 November.

Gianini, Paul. 1998. "Moving from Innovation to Transformation in the Community College." *Leadership Abstracts* (October).

Gladieux, Lawrence E., and Watson Scott Swail. 1999. *The Virtual University and Educational Opportunity: Issues of Equity and Access for the Next Generation.* Washington, D.C.: The College Board. ERIC No. ED 428 637.

Gleazer, Edmund J., Jr. 1998a. "Reflections on Values and Vitality: Perspectives for the 21st Century." Presentation at 1998 Community College Futures Assembly, 2 March, Orlando, Fla.

———. 1998b. Letter to New Expeditions Project, 1 September.

Governor's 2020 Commission on the Future of Post-Secondary Education. 1998. *Learning for Life: Report of the 2020 Commission on the Future of Post-Secondary Education.* Olympia, Wash.: Governor's Executive Policy Office.

Grubb, W. Norton. 1998. Letter to New Expeditions Project, 23 July.

———. 1999. *Learning and Earning in the Middle: The Economic Benefits of Sub-Baccalaureate Education.* New York: Community College Research Center, Institute on Education and the Economy/Teachers College, Columbia University. ERIC No. ED 431 459.

Heelan, Cynthia, Judith Redwine, and Antonia Black. 1999. "Community Colleges as the Laboratory for a New Form of Democracy: Synocracy." Draft paper, 30 March.

Hockaday, Jeff, and Donald E. Puyear. 2000. *Community College Leadership in the New Millennium.* New Expeditions Issues Paper Series, no. 8. Washington, D.C.: Community College Press, American Association of Community Colleges.

Hodgkinson, Harold (Bud). 1998. Letter to New Expeditions Project, 13 September.

Holmes, William. 1999. "The Transforming Power of Information Technology." *Community College Journal* 70 (October/November): 10–15.

Immerwahr, John. 1999. *Taking Responsibility: Leaders' Expectations of Higher Education.* Washington, D.C.: National Center for Public Policy and Higher Education.

Ingram, Richard T. 1997. *Transforming Public Trusteeship.* AGB Public Policy Paper Series, no. 97-2. Washington, D.C.: Association of Governing Boards of Universities and Colleges. ERIC No. ED 412 831.

Jurow, Susan, and John Quinley. 1998. *Recruiting and Retaining Quality Faculty in Corporate and Continuing Education: A Critical Challenge for Continuing Education and Training and Human Resource Professionals.* Washington, D.C.: The College and University Personnel Association.

Kee, Arnold. 1999. Memorandum to New Expeditions Project, 11 June.

Kellogg Commission on the Future of State and Land-Grant Universities. 1998. *Returning to Our Roots: Student Access, Second Report.* Washington, D.C.: Kellogg Commission on the Future of State and Land-Grant Universities. ERIC No. ED 419 467.

Kelly, J. Terence. 1998. Letter to New Expeditions Project, 6 November.

King, Charles R. 1998. Letter to New Expeditions Project, 6 November.

Kopischke, Kevin J. 1996. "Responding to a New Customer of Higher Education Determining the Learning Needs and Expectations of Business and Industry Customers and the Incumbent Workforce." Ph.D. diss., University of Minnesota.

Kull, Michael and William E. Halal. 1999. "The Technology Revolution: The George Washington University Forecast of Emerging Technologies." *On the Horizon* 7 (1). Internet: http://horizon.unc.edu/horizon/online/html/7/1/ [Accessed: 27 October 1999].

Laird, E., 1999. "Distance Learning Instructors: Watch Out for the Cutting Edge," *Chronicle of Higher Education,* 28 May, B6.

Maeroff, Gene I. 1998. Letter to New Expeditions Project, 9 July.

Maier, Steve. 1998. "Ideas for a New Decade." E-mail to New Expeditions Project, 4 November.

Maricopa Community College Governing Board. 1999. "Strategic Issues Regarding Funding and FTSE." Strategic conversation held by Maricopa Community College Governing Board, 8 June, Phoenix.

Mast, Linda, et al. 1999. "Collaboration in a Competitive Environment: A Unique Partnership to Train Allied Health Professionals." Forum at the 79th Annual Convention of American Association of Community Colleges, 8 April, Nashville.

McCabe, Robert H., and Philip R. Day Jr. 1998. *Developmental Education: A Twenty-First Century Social and Economic Imperative.* Mission Viejo, Calif.: League for Innovation in the Community College and The College Board. ERIC No. ED 421 176.

McDonald, Patricia A. 1998. Letter to New Expeditions Project, 10 November.

MDC, Inc. 1998. "Statement for the Record on Rural Community Colleges by MDC, Inc., for the New Expeditions Project." 1 December. Typescript.

Mellow, Gail O., Julius Sokenu, and Brian Lynch-Donohue. 1998. "Integrating Technology into the Classroom: Exploring What It Means for Faculty and Students." *Community College Journal* 69 (August/September): 24–30.

Merisotis, Jamie P., and Thomas R. Wolanin. 2000. *Community College Financing: Strategies and Challenges.* New Expeditions Issues Paper Series, no. 5. Washington, D.C.: Community College Press, American Association of Community Colleges.

Milliron, Mark D., and Ernest R. Leach. 1997. "Community Colleges Winning through Innovation: Taking on the Changes and Choices of Leadership in the Twenty-First Century." In *Leadership Abstracts.* Special Edition. Mission Viejo, Calif.: League for Innovation in the Community College.

Mohraz, Judy Jolley. 2000. "Missing Men on Campus." *The Washington Post,* 15 January, B7.

National Council on Student Development. 1999. "Results of NCSD Survey on New Expeditions Project on Most Critical Issues Facing Community Colleges." Quincy, Ill.: National Council on Student Development. Typescript.

"National Postsecondary Student Aid Study: 1995-96 (NPSAS:96)." Data set. Washington, D.C.: National Center for Education Statistics, U.S. Dept. of Education.

National Telecommunications and Information Administration (NTIA). 1999. *Falling through the Net: Defining the Digital Divide.* Washington, D.C.: U.S. Department of Commerce. Internet: www.ntia.doc.gov/ntiahome/fttn99/contents.html.

Nettles, Michael T., and Catherine M. Millett. 2000. *Student Access in Community Colleges.* New Expeditions Issues Paper Series, no. 1. Washington, D.C.: Community College Press, American Association of Community Colleges.

Nevada Community College Futures Commission Committee. 1991. *Futures Commission Report: Changing with the Times, Challenging the Future.* Reno: Nevada Community College Futures Commission Committee. ERIC No. ED 355 985.

Nielsen, Norm. 1996. Letter and materials to New Expeditions Project, November.

Nora, Amaury. 2000. *Reexamining the Community College Mission.* New Expeditions Issues Paper Series, no. 2. Washington, D.C.: Community College Press, American Association of Community Colleges.

O'Banion, Terry. 1997. *A Learning College for the 21st Century.* Phoenix: Oryx Press

Olsen, Florence. 1999. "Faculty Wariness of Technology Remains a Challenge, Computing Survey Finds." *Chronicle of Higher Education,* 29 October, A65.

Packer, Arnold. 1998. "The End of Routine Work and the Need for a Career Transcript." Indianapolis: Hudson Institute.

Padrón, Eduardo. 1998. Letter to New Expeditions Project, 10 November.

Page, Clarence. 1999. "Inclusiveness: Current Affairs in America." Speech at the 79th Annual Convention of American Association of Community Colleges, 8 April, Nashville.

Parnell, Dale. 1998a. Letter to New Expeditions Project, 5 August.

———. 1998b. "Removing the Hourglass Approach to Education." In *Tech Prep: The Next Generation,* eds. Dan Hull and Julie Grevelle. Waco, Tex.: Center for Occupational Research and Development.

Pascarella, Ernest T. 1999. "New Studies Track Community College Effects on Students." *Community College Journal* 69 (June/July): 8–14.

Pasch, Rodney G. 1998. Letter and materials to New Expeditions Project, 11 November.

Perin, Dolores. 1998. *Curriculum and Pedagogy to Integrate Occupational and Academic Instruction in the Community College: Implications for Faculty Development.* New York: Community College Research Center, Institute on Education and the

Economy/Teachers College, Columbia University. ERIC No. ED 428 793.

Phelps, Donald G. 1994. "What Lies Ahead for Community Colleges as We Hurtle Toward the 21st Century?" *Community College Journal* 65 (August/September): 22–25.

Phillippe, Kent A., and Madeline Patton. 2000. *National Profile of Community Colleges: Trends and Statistics.* 3d ed. Washington, D.C.: Community College Press, American Association of Community Colleges.

Phipps, Ronald. 1998. *College Remediation: What It Is, What It Costs, What's at Stake.* Washington, D.C.: The Institute for Higher Education Policy. ERIC No. ED 429 525.

Purdy, Leslie. 1998. Letter to New Expeditions Project, 16 November.

Puyear, Donald E. 1998. "Community Colleges in 2010." Draft paper, State Board of Directors for Community Colleges of Arizona, Phoenix.

Quinley, John W., and Melissa Quinley. 1998. *Four-Year Graduates Attending Community Colleges: A New Meaning for the Term "Second Chance."* New York: Community College Research Center, Institute on Education and the Economy/Teachers College, Columbia University. ERIC No. ED 428 790.

Raisman, Neal. 1998. "Doing Education with Business and the Middle Child Syndrome: Promise or Threat to the Community College Mission." Draft paper, Onondaga Community College, Syracuse, N.Y.

Rendón, Laura. 2000. *Fulfilling the Promise of Access and Opportunity: Collaborative Community Colleges for the 21st Century.* New Expeditions Issues Paper Series, no. 3. Washington, D.C.: Community College Press, American Association of Community Colleges.

Rifkin, Tronie. 2000. *Public Community College Faculty.* New Expeditions Issues Paper Series, no. 4. Washington, D.C.: Community College Press, American Association of Community Colleges.

Risley, Rod. 1998. Interview by Madeline Patton, 6 October.

Romero, Martha. 1998. Letter to New Expeditions Project, 8 December.

Rosenbaum, J. E. 1998. *Unrealistic Plans and Misdirected Efforts: Are Community Colleges Getting the Right Message to High School Students?* New York: Community College Research Center, Institute on Education and the Economy/Teachers College, Columbia University. ERIC No. ED 428 795.

Roueche, John .E. and Suanne.D. Roueche. 1999a. *High Stakes, High Performance: Making Remedial Education Work.* Washington, D.C.: Community College Press, American Association of Community Colleges.

———.1999b. Speech at 79th Annual Convention of American Association of Community Colleges, 9 April, Nashville.

Rowe, Drew. 1999. "Teaching with Technology: A Faculty Development Approach." *Community College Journal* 70 (October/November): 24–30.

Ryland, Jane N. 2000. *Technology and the Future of the Community College.* New Expeditions Issues Paper Series, no. 10. Washington, D.C.: Community College Press, American Association of Community Colleges.

Salter, Linda G. 1999. "Down in the Valley." *Community College Journal* 70 (October/November): 37–41.

Secretary's Commission on Achieving Necessary Skills (SCANS). 1992. *Learning a Living: A Blueprint for High Performance.* Washington, D.C.: U.S. Department of Labor. Internet: www.ttrc.doleta.gov/scans/scans3.html.

Skills 2000 Commission. 1998. *Skills 2000 Commission Report: Major Employers' Assessment of their Employment and Skills Needs to Year 2005.* Des Moines, Iowa: Skills 2000 Commission.

Southern Education Foundation. 1998. *Miles to Go: A Report on Black Students and Postsecondary Education in the South.* Atlanta: Southern Education Foundation. ERIC No. ED 426 132.

Suplee, Curt. 2000. "Imagine This." *The Washington Post*, 2 January, B1–3.

Theobald, Robert. 1994. "What Does the 21st Century Hold for Community Colleges?" *Community College Journal* 65 (August/September): 16–21.

Transue, Pamela J. 1998. Letter to New Expeditions Project, 4 November.

Traub, James. 1999. "The End of Affirmative Action (and the Beginning of Something Better)." *The New York Times Magazine*, 2 May, 44–51, 76, 78–79.

21st Century Skills Leadership Group. 1999. *Report of the 21st Century Skills Leadership Group to Vice President Gore.* Washington, D.C.: 21st Century Skills Leadership Group.

University and Community College System of Nevada Board of Regents. 1998. *Strategic Directions for the University and Community College System of Nevada.* Reno: University and Community College System of Nevada Board of Regents.

Walker, Kenneth P. 1997. "Should Community Colleges Offer Bachelor's Degrees?" *Community College Times*, 5 November.

Warfield, Marji Erickson, et al. "Adaptation during Early Childhood among Mothers of Children with Disabilities." 1999. *Journal of Developmental and Behavioral Pediatrics* 20: 14–19.

Wattenbarger, James L. 1998. Letter to New Expeditions Project, 30 August.

Wellman, J. V. 1999. "Contributing to the Civic Good: Assessing and Accounting for the Civic Contributions of Higher Education." Working paper, The New Millennium Project on Higher Education Costs, Pricing and Productivity, The Institute for Higher Education Policy, Washington, D.C.

Whitehead, Ronald. 1999. Interview by Madeline Patton, May.

"The Wired Society: A Harvard Magazine Roundtable." *Harvard Magazine* 101 (May-June): 42–53, 106–107. Cambridge, Mass.: Harvard University.

Contributors

The following organizations sponsored public hearings, focus groups, and community conversations, in coordination with or in addition to AACC and ACCT:

American Council on International Intercultural Education, Des Plaines, Ill.

American Indian Higher Education Consortium, Alexandria, Va.

Association of College Unions International, Bloomington, Ind.

Bronx Community College, Bronx, N.Y.

Cedar Valley College, Lancaster, Tex.

Community Colleges for International Development, Cedar Rapids, Iowa

Consortium for Community College Development, University of Michigan, Ann Arbor

Council for Resource Development, Washington, D.C.

ERIC Clearinghouse for Community Colleges, Los Angeles

Foothill College, Los Altos Hills, Calif.

Ford Foundation, New York

Frederick Community College, Frederick, Md.

Institute of Higher Education, University of Florida, Gainesville

Instructional Telecommunications Council, Washington, D.C.

League for Innovation in the Community Colleges, Mission Viejo, Calif.

National Council for Continuing Education and Training, Eugene, Oreg.

National Institute for Staff and Organizational Development, Austin, Tex.

National Society for Experiential Education, Alexandria, Va.

Owens Community College, Toledo, Ohio

Palomar College, San Marcos, Calif.

Phi Theta Kappa, Jackson, Miss.

Rural Community College Initiative, MDC, Inc., Chapel Hill, N.C.

The Stanley Foundation, Muscatine, Iowa

University of Florida, Gainesville

The following people contributed papers and comments:

Cliff Adelman, U.S. Department of Education, Washington, D.C.

Brenda Norman Albright, Franklin Education Group, Franklin, Tenn.

Richard Alfred, University of Michigan, Ann Arbor

George Autry, MDC, Inc., Chapel Hill, N.C.

George A. Baker, North Carolina State University, Raleigh

Thomas E. Barton, Greenville Technical College, Greenville, S.C.

Ann Beheler, Richland College, Dallas

Trudy Bers, Oakton College, Des Plaines, Ill.

Antonia Black, Regis University, Denver

Vivian B. Blevins, St. Louis Community College

George R. Boggs, Palomar College, San Marcos, Calif.

Joseph A. Borgen, Des Moines Area Community College, Ankeny, Iowa

Peter D. Boyse, Delta College, University Center, Mich.

Clifford M. Brock, Bainbridge College, Bainbridge, Ga.

David Buettner, North Iowa Area Community College, Mason City

Peter F. Burnham, Brookdale Community College, Lincroft, N.J.

Anthony D. Calabro, University and Community College System of Nevada, Reno

Anthony P. Carnevale, Educational Testing Service, Washington, D.C.

Patricia Carter, University of Michigan, Ann Arbor

C. E. Chiesi, Harford Community College, Bel Air, Md.

Dennis Christensen, Central Wyoming College, Riverton

Willard R. Daggett, International Center for Leadership in Education, Inc., Schenectady, N.Y.

Gary Davis, Illinois Community College Trustees Association

Judith S. Eaton, Council for Higher Education Accreditation, Washington, DC

Allen Edwards, Pellissippi State Technical Community College, Knoxville, Tenn.

Steve Eskow, The Electronic University Network, San Francisco and Orlando, Fla.

Sean A. Fanelli, Nassau Community College, Garden City, N.Y.

Richard L. Ferguson, ACT, Inc., Iowa City, Iowa

William J. Flynn, Palomar College, San Marcos, Calif.

Norman Fortenberry, National Science Foundation, Arlington, Va.

Thomas E. Gamble, Joliet Junior College, Joliet, Ill.

Leonardo de la Garza, Tarrant County College, Fort Worth, Tex.

Edmund J. Gleazer, Bethesda, Md.

Sharon Gordon, Port of Portland, Portland, Oreg.

W. Norton Grubb, University of California at Berkeley, Berkeley, Calif.

Samuel Halperin, American Youth Policy Forum, Washington, D.C.

Ray Hancock, John A. Logan College, Carterville, Ill.

Cynthia Heelan, Colorado Mountain College, Glenwood Springs, Colo.

Carl Hite, Cleveland State Community College, Cleveland, Tenn.

Jeff Hockaday, Cary, N.C.

Harold Hodgkinson, Center for Demographic Policy, Institute for Educational Leadership, Washington, D.C.

Richard T. Ingram, Association of Governing Boards of Universities and Colleges, Washington, D.C.

Earl P. Johnson, San Mateo County Community College District, San Mateo, Calif.

Arnold M. Kee, American Association of Community Colleges, Washington, D.C.

J. Terence Kelly, Delgado Community College, New Orleans

Charles R. King, Southwest Virginia Community College, Richlands, Va.

Kevin J. Kopischke, Alexandria Technical College, Alexandria, Minn.

John P. Kristofco, Wayne College, University of Akron, Orrville, Ohio

Eric Larson, Blackhawk Technical College, Janesville, Wis.

Dave Leo, Net1Plus, Lunenberg, Mass.

Jack M. Lewis, New River Community College, Dublin, Va.

Harold Loyd, Abraham Baldwin Agriculture College, Tifton, Ga.

Gene Maeroff, Teachers College, Columbia University, New York

Stephen J. Maier, Sheridan College, Sheridan, Wyo.

Robert McCabe, League for Innovation in the Community College, Miami, Fla.

Patricia A. McDonald, Community College of Allegheny County, Pittsburgh

Polly McMahon, Spokane Falls Community College, Spokane, Wash.

Jamie P. Merisotis, The Institute for Higher Education Policy, Washington, D.C.

Catherine M. Millett, University of Michigan, Ann Arbor

Kenneth J. Minnaert, South Puget Sound Community College, Olympia, Wash.

Louise Mirrer, The City University of New York, New York

Michael T. Nettles, University of Michigan, Ann Arbor

Norm Nielsen, Kirkwood Community College, Cedar Rapids, Iowa

Amaury Nora, University of Houston, Houston, Tex.

Terry O'Banion, League for Innovation in the Community College, Mission Viejo, Calif.

Eduardo Padrón, Miami-Dade Community College, Miami, Fla.

Dale Parnell, Redmond, Oreg.

Rodney G. Pasch, Moraine Park Technical College, Fond du Lac, Wis.

Marie Pepicello, Phoenix College, Phoenix

Dan Phelan, Southeastern Community College, West Burlington, Iowa

Leslie Purdy, Coastline Community College, Fountain Valley, Calif.

Donald E. Puyear, State Board of Directors for Community Colleges of Arizona, Phoenix

Neal Raisman, Academic Marketing and Positioning Solutions, Jamesville, N.Y.

Lee Rasch, Western Wisconsin Technical College, La Crosse

Judith Redwine, State Center Community College District, Fresno, Calif.

Don Reichard, James Sprunt Community College, Kenansville, N.C.

Laura Rendón, California State University, Long Beach

Tronie Rifkin, Evaluation and Training Institute, Los Angeles

Rod Risley, Phi Theta Kappa, Jackson, Miss.

Carl Rolf, Northwest Iowa Community College, Sheldon

Richard M. Romano, The Institute for Community College Research, Broome Community College, Binghamton, N.Y.

Martha Romero, Siskiyou Joint Community College District, Weed, Calif.

Richard Rouillard, Oklahoma City Community College, Oklahoma City

Jane N. Ryland, President Emerita, CAUSE

Susan A. Smith, Midlands Technical College, Columbia, S.C.

Donald Stewart, The College Board, New York

Donald Supalla, Rochester Community and Technical College, Rochester, Minn.

Roberta Teahen, Northwestern Michigan College, Traverse City, Mich.

Jeri Thornton, Oklahoma State University-Oklahoma City

Pamela J. Transue, Tacoma Community College, Tacoma, Wash.

Scott Vettleson, Litchfield High School, Litchfield, Minn.

Kenneth P. Walker, Edison Community College, Fort Myers, Fla.

James L. Wattenbarger, Gainesville, Fla.

James F. Weber, Arapahoe Community College, Littleton, Colo.

Ronald Whitehead, Jones County Junior College, Ellisville, Miss.

Kathleen A. Williams, The Boeing Company, Seattle

Thomas R. Wolanin, The Institute for Higher Education Policy, Washington, D.C.

Index

The following New Expeditions issues papers
are available as a set from Community College Press®:

Student Access in Community Colleges, by Michael T. Nettles and Catherine M. Millett

Reexamining the Community College Mission, by Amaury Nora

Fulfilling the Promise of Access and Opportunity:
Collaborative Community Colleges for the 21st Century, by Laura Rendón

Public Community College Faculty, by Tronie Rifkin

Community College Financing: Strategies and Challenges,
by Jamie P. Merisotis and Thomas R. Wolanin

Contradictory Colleges: Thriving in an Era of Continuous Change,
by Richard Alfred and Patricia Carter

Issues in Community College Governance, by Gary Davis

Community College Leadership in the New Millennium,
by Jeff Hockaday and Donald E. Puyear

The Search for the Learning-Centered College, by William Flynn

Technology and the Future of the Community College, by Jane N. Ryland

Community Colleges and Career Qualifications, by Anthony P. Carnevale

Charting the Future of Global Education in Community Colleges,
by the American Council on International Intercultural Education,
Community Colleges for International Development, and The Stanley Foundation

To purchase the set of 12 papers (order #1523) or the report,
The Knowledge Net (order # 1436), please contact

Community College Press
P.O. Box 311
Annapolis Junction, Maryland 20701-0311
Phone: (800) 250-6557
Fax: (301) 604-0158
E-mail: aaccpub@pmds.com
www.aacc.nche.edu/bookstore